Fiddle Time Starters

a beginner book for violin

Kathy and David Blackwell

Illustrations by

Martin Remphry

T0057020

MUSIC DEPARTMENT

OXFORD
UNIVERSITY PRESS

Great Clarendon Street, Oxford OX2 6DP, England

This collection © Oxford University Press 2012
All pieces (music and words) are by Kathy and David Blackwell
and are © Oxford University Press, apart from:

- Traditional melodies: CD tracks 2, 6, 9, 31, 33–6, 43–4, and 66 (words and arrangement © Oxford University Press);
- Traditional words: CD tracks 10, 34, and 35–6;
- Composed melodies: CD tracks 17, 22, and 41 (arrangement © Oxford University Press).

Unauthorized arrangement or photocopying of this copyright material is **ILLEGAL**.

Kathy and David Blackwell have asserted their right under the Copyright, Designs
and Patents Act, 1988, to be identified as the Composers of this Work.

ISBN 978-0-19-336584-1

Music and text origination by Julia Bovee

Welcome to **Fiddle Time Starters**. You'll find:

- Lots of tunes to sing and then play
- A lively CD to listen and play along to
- Quizzes to do—grab a pencil
- 'Super listener' games—get your ears ready
- 'Be a composer' activities—get creative!

What you'll need:

Violin

Fingers and short fingernails

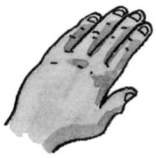

Rosin

Bow

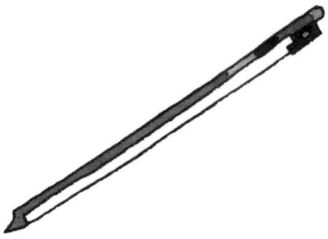

Pencil

CD player

Got these? Let's get started.

Tune your strings to tracks 71–4 (A, D, G, E).

This book belongs to _____

Feel the beat

1 Music has a steady beat, can you feel it in your feet?

1 2 3 4 5 6 7 8

(*stamp feet*)

Hear the music in the band, can you feel it in your hands?

1 2 3 4 5 6 7 8

(*clap hands*)

Now let's try a clever trick, can you make your fingers click?

1 2 3 4 5 6 7 8

(*click fingers*)

'Feel the beat' is what I said, can you think it in your head?

(1) (2) (3) (4) (5) (6) (7) **8**

(*count silently until beat eight*)

Music has a steady beat or pulse. Just like your heartbeat, it keeps going all the way through a song or tune. A fast tune will have a fast beat and a slower tune a slower beat.

Tap a steady beat and chant the words of a song you know well. Keep tapping all the way through.

Know your violin

2 Song time

Sing these words to the tune of 'Head, shoulders, knees, and toes' and point to the different parts of your instrument.

Scroll, shoulders, strings, and bridge, strings and bridge,
Scroll, shoulders, strings, and bridge, strings and bridge,
* And the pegs and chin-rest and the fingerboard,
Scroll, shoulders, strings, and bridge, strings and bridge.

* **Verse 2**: And the nut and *f* holes and the tail-piece,

Picture time

Draw a line from each word to the correct part of the violin.

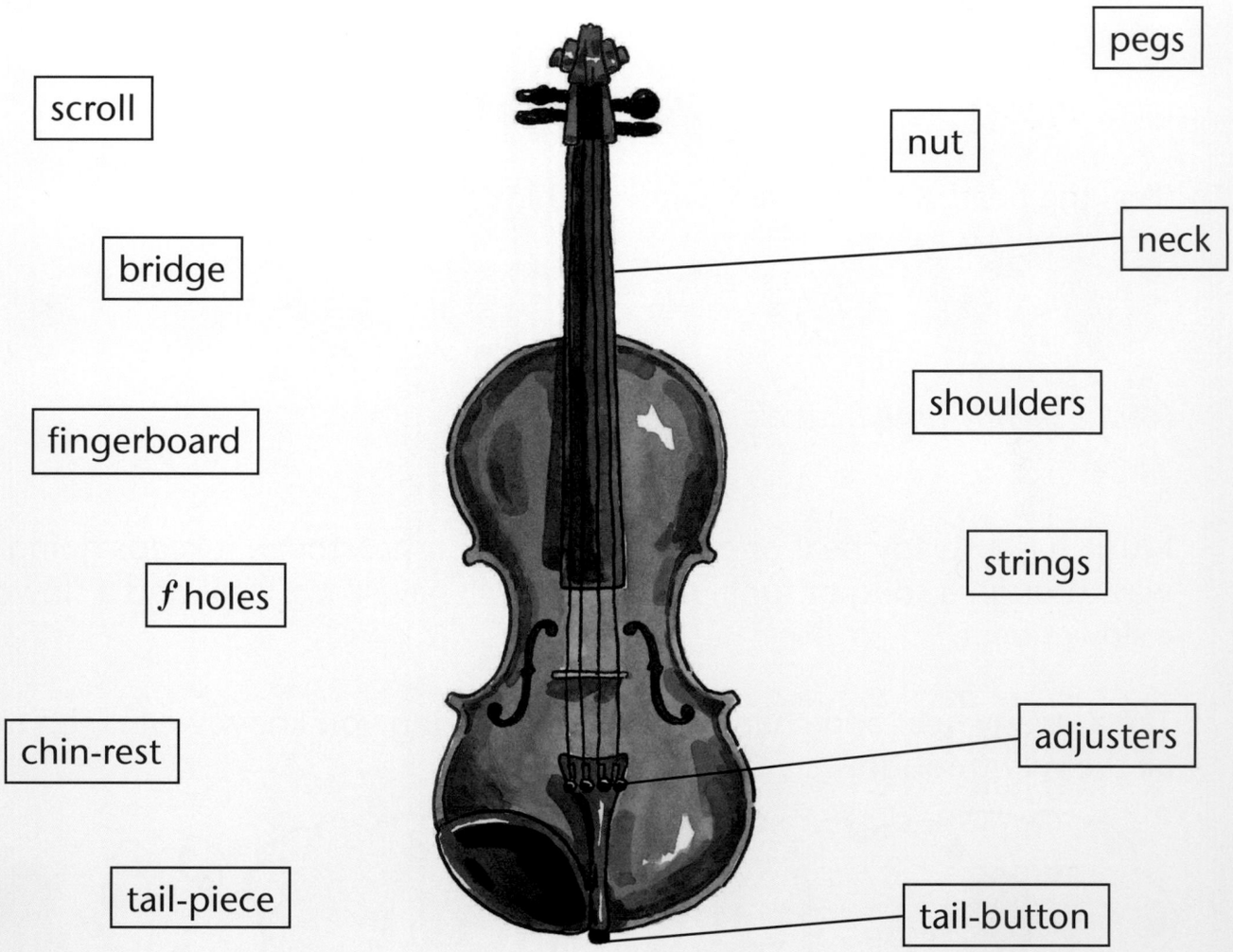

3 Get-ready rag

Stand with your feet slightly apart and get ready to do each of the actions along with the CD. For 5–8, hold your violin steady with your right hand while you move to the music.

1. Rest position now,

2. Hold it out in front,

3. Lift it up on high,

4. On your shoulder now.

5. **Feel the beat**: sway on the spot, left and right.
6. **Swinging hammock**: swing your elbows.
7. **High jump**: tap your left hand on the strings or the wood either side of the fingerboard.
8. **Long jump**: slide your left hand up and down the fingerboard.

First sounds

In these tunes, pluck the open strings with your right-hand fingers. Make a big circle in the air with your right arm, like this:

4 Sway and strum

Sway gently from side to side in time to the music while you strum the strings.

Strum... strum... etc.

5 At the zoo

Listen to the sound of each string, then play the note pizzicato—that means plucking.

Listen		*Play and chant*	
E	for elephants	E	for elephants
A	for alligators	A	for alligators
D	for dolphins	D	for dolphins
G	for gorillas	G	for gorillas

Chant

That's what we have in our zoo. Yeah!

6 Swing, swing, swing your arm

Sing and then play this piece to the tune of 'Row, row, row your boat'.

G G G D

Swing, swing, swing your arm, as we sing this song.

x2

G G D G

Swing it out and swing it in, we'll swing it all day long.

7 Flying around

E A

Swing with your arm as you

D G

pluck ev - 'ry string.

E A

Fly - ing a - round is a

D G

won - der - ful thing!

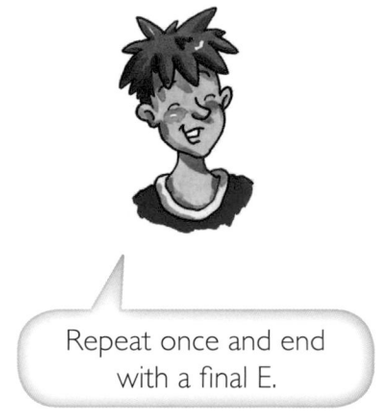

First tunes

Play these tunes pizzicato, placing your thumb on the edge of the fingerboard.

8 Counting beats

Play this piece four times, once with each string.

Chant

Counting beats is for the best, play four Gs* then count four rests.

Play x4

G G G G ≀ ≀ ≀ ≀

* then D, A, and E

9 The drunken sailor

Sing

Let's all play pizzicato, let's all play pizzicato,
Let's all play pizzicato, early in the morning.

Play

D D D D G G G G

D D D D G G D D x2

10 Jelly on a plate

DD	AA	D	≀	DD	AA	D	≀
Jelly	on a	plate,	(rest)	Jelly	on a	plate,	(rest)

DD	DD	AA	AA	DD	AA	D	≀
Wibble	wobble,	wibble	wobble,	Jelly	on a	plate.	(rest)

x2

Super listener

When you can sing and then play 'Jelly on a plate' really well, try a high version starting on the A string. Then play a low version—which string will you begin on?

Be a composer

1. Make up your own tune by playing the pattern of the following words on your open strings. Tap a steady beat and say the words through a few times before you start.

'I hear footsteps on the street.
Someone's there with great big feet!'

2. Invent your own tune using notes from the boxes. Write your tune in the heartbeat spaces—one box per heartbeat—and then play it from start to finish.

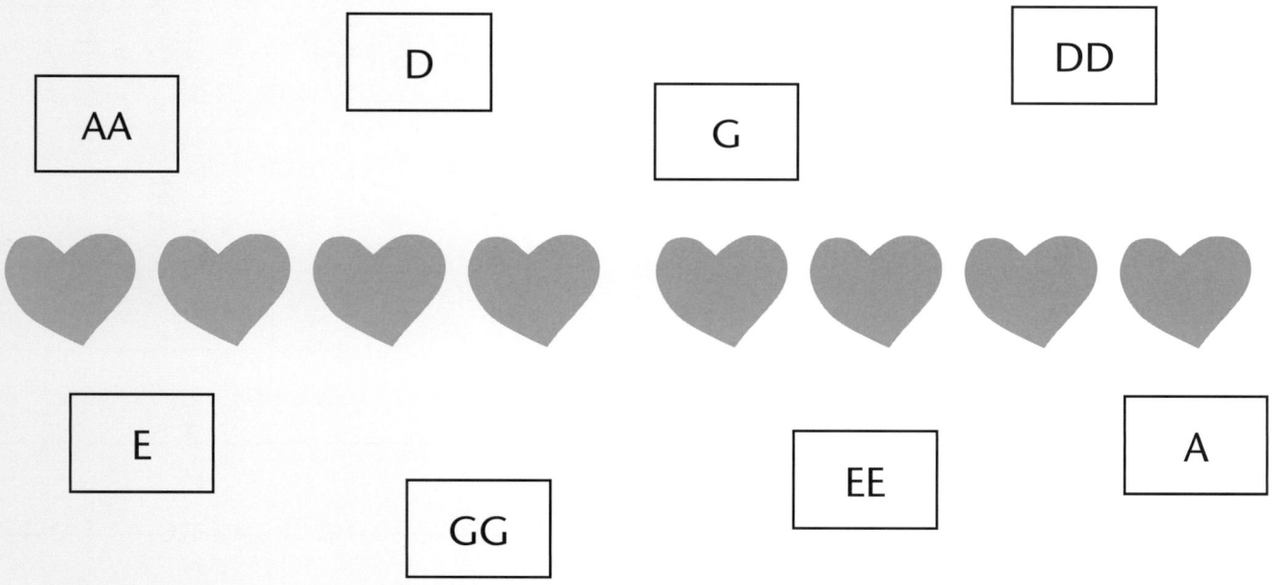

Give your tune a title: _____

Know your bow

11 Song time

Sing these words along with the CD and point to the different parts of the bow.

1. There's the point and the heel and the stick in between,
   Don't touch the hair to keep it clean.

2. Turn the screw to the right to make the hair tight,
   Rosin the bow and off we go.

3. Turn the screw to the left to loosen the bow,
   That's what we do when it's time to go.

Picture time

Draw a line from each word to the correct part of the bow.

stick

point (tip)

screw

heel (frog)

hair

Quiz time

What am I?

You turn me to loosen and tighten the hair of the bow: _____

I'm part of the bow that you don't touch: _____

You rub me on the hair before you play: _____

You'll find the heel at one end of the bow and me at the other end: _____

12 Yo bow!

Get ready to perform this bow-hold rap by holding the middle of the stick with your left hand. The tip of the bow will point to your left.

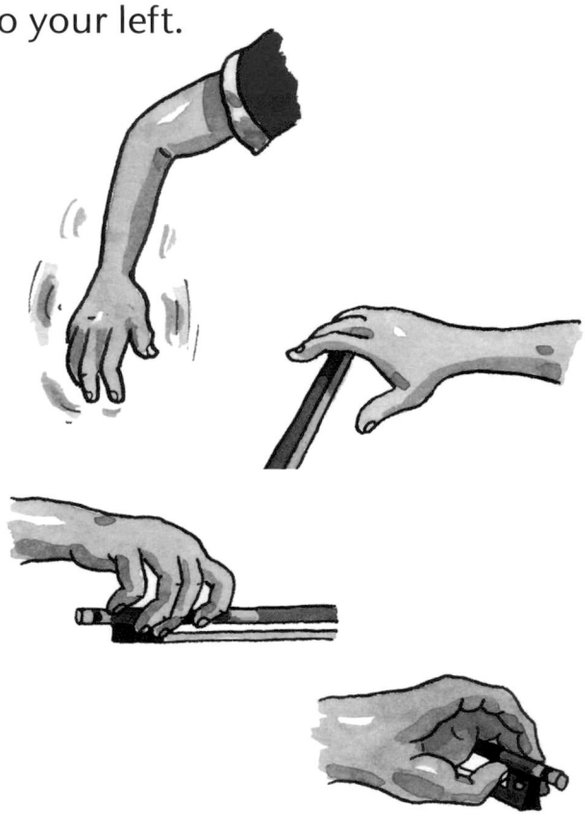

1. Shake your right hand to the ground,
   Wiggle those fingers all around.

2. Hang your fingers right over the stick,
   Slightly apart now, that's the trick.

3. Lean your hand, don't let it drop,
   Put your little finger right on top.

4. Bend your thumb and bring it round,
   Keep it curved to make a great sound.

5. Yo bow! Yo bow!
   To the left, to the right, and off we go.

6. Yo bow! Yo bow!
   Up and down and off we go.

7. Yo bow! Yo bow!
   Round and round and off we go.

8. Yo bow! Yo bow!
   Side to side and off we go.

Down- and up-bow signs

⊓ This is a down-bow sign—pull your right hand away from the strings.
V This is an up-bow sign—push your right hand up towards the strings.

Play this pattern on each open string: ⊓ V ⊓ V
down up down up

Following the signs

Choose one of these patterns and play it a few times on an open string.

	⊓	V	⊓	𝄾	V	⊓	V	𝄾
1.	What	goes	down,	(rest)	then	goes	up!	(rest)
	V	⊓	V	𝄾	⊓	V	⊓	𝄾
2.	Up	bows	push,	(rest)	down	bows	pull!	(rest)
	⊓	V	⊓	V	⊓	V	⊓	𝄾
3.	Out	in	out	in	out	in	out.	(rest)
	⊓	V	𝄾	𝄾	⊓	V	𝄾	𝄾
4.	Down	up	(rest)	(rest)	down	up.	(rest)	(rest)

Try the same patterns on your rosin. Make sure the bow moves and not the rosin!

Now play the tunes on page 8 arco—that means with the bow. For 'The drunken sailor', change the words to 'Let's all play arco'.

Rhythm zone 1: walk, jogging

'walk'
crotchet (or quarter-note)

'jogging'
quavers (or eighth-notes)

- Clap the rhythms below, saying 'walk' for each ♩ and 'jogging' for each ♫
- Ask someone to tap the beat while you clap the rhythms, and then swap.
- Choose one row of beats (a bar or measure) and play that rhythm on each open string. For Set 1, count a steady **1**-2-3-4, **1**-2-3-4 before you start. For Set 2, count **1**-2-3, **1**-2-3.
- Finally, play each ♩ on the E string and each ♫ on the A string, or choose two other strings that are next to each other.

$\frac{4}{4}$ is a **time signature**. It means four ♩ beats in each bar.

What do you think $\frac{3}{4}$ means?

Set 1

Set 2

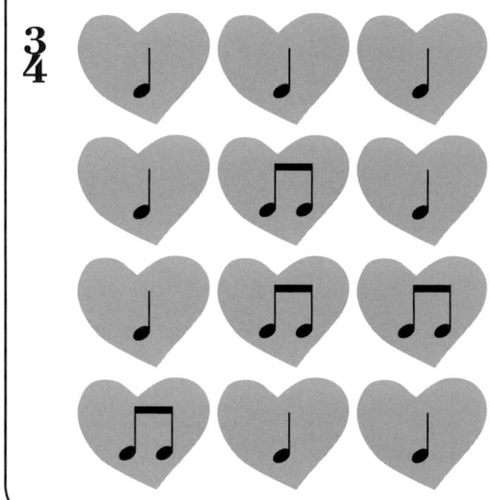

13 Super listener

Listen to track 13, 'Echo calypso', and copy back the rhythms on the D and A strings.

Notes on the stave

14 Open-string rap

Chant

Violin strings from high to low, let me tell you how they go.
First there's E then A then D, way down low you'll find the G.
E A D G. Way down low you'll find the G.

Play each string from high to low, start with E and down you go.

Play

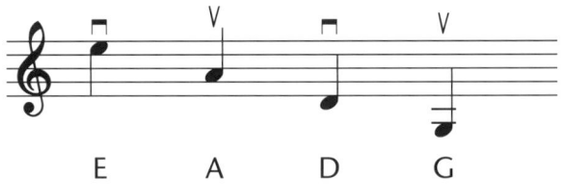

Chant

Play each string from low to high, start with G then reach for the sky!

Play

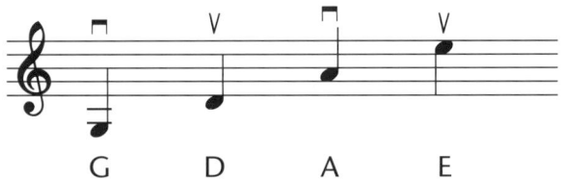

Quiz time

Draw the correct open string above each letter to spell the words as notes.

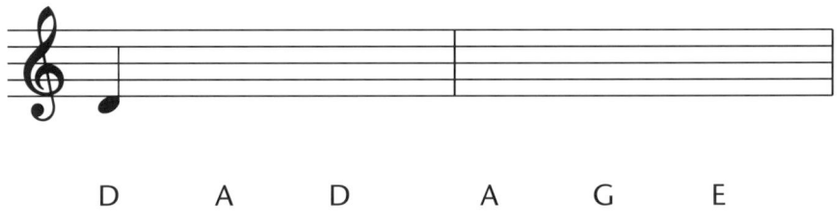

What words do these notes spell? Fill in the name of each string to find out.

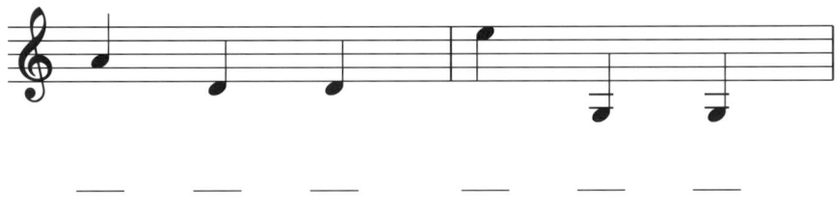

Walk and jogging tunes

15 At the zoo

Listen *Copy* (etc.)

E for e - le - phants, E for e - le - phants,

A for al - li - ga - tors, A for al - li - ga - tors,

D for dol - phins, D for dol - phins,

G for go - ril - las, G for go - ril - las,

Chant

That's what we have in our zoo. Yeah!

This is a barline: It divides music into bars.

A double barline comes at the end of a tune:

Be a composer

Make up your own rhythms using the open strings. Think of something beginning with each letter and then play the pattern of the words on each string. You could use the names of friends or different places as starting points. Write your words in the spaces below:

E for _____

A for _____

D for _____

G for _____

16 Copycat blues

Driving

Listen *Copy* (etc.)

D D

G D

A G

D A

When the music repeats, the rhythm is different—it sounds like 'We are the champions!'. Listen carefully and copy what you hear.

17 Mini Mozart

This is a repeat sign:

Gracefully

Mozart, arr. KB/DB

Mo - zart, Mo - zart, etc.

Try these rhythm variations:

etc.

Wolf-gang A - ma - de - us, Wolf-gang A - ma - de - us,

etc.

Walk jog - ging walk, walk jog - ging walk,

etc.

Pull to the tip then push to the heel then

18 Boogie band

With energy

Boo-gie on the o-pen D, boo-gie on the o-pen G, boo-gie on the o-pen D,

boo-gie on the A. Boo-gie on the o-pen D, boo-gie on the o-pen G,

boo-gie on the D then G. Yeah!

19 Rhythm train

Verse 1

Lively

O-ver-night ex-press train, O-ver-night ex-press train, etc.

Verse 2

All a-board, all a-board, All a-board, all a-board,

Verse 3

Train whis-tle, train whis-tle, Train whis-tle, train whis-tle,

20 Super listener

Listen to track 20 and play 'Rhythm train' using your G and D strings.

21 Mr Pizzicato and friends

Sing the words and play the notes in each verse.

Verse 1

Mr Pizzicato likes to pluck the string, he puts his finger here and he lets it ring:

Mr Pizzicato likes to pluck the string.

Verse 2

Mr Arco has a great bow-hold, he strokes the strings and it sounds so bold:

Mr Arco has a great bow-hold.

Verse 3

Mr Col Legno likes to use the wood, he bounces very gently and it sounds real good:

Mr Col Legno likes to use the wood.

Verse 4

Mr Tremolo likes to shiver with his bow, so he puts it near the tip and this is how it goes:

Mr Tremolo likes to shiver with his bow.

End the song with tremolo on the D string.

Use your new tremolo skills to play a spooky version of 'The drunken sailor' on page 8. Change the words to 'Let's all play with tremolo bowing'.

String-crossing tunes

In these string-crossing tunes, watch your elbow swing *up* when you play a lower string and *down* when you play a higher string.

22 Happy Haydn

Simply

Haydn, arr. KB/DB

When you cross from string to string, watch your el - bow do a swing.

Make it do that swing-ing thing, when you cross a string.

Are you using your elbow to help you move from string to string?

This means you should rest for two beats: –

23 Monkeys swing

Rock groove

Mon-keys swing from tree to tree, they swing so fast they might catch me, hey!

1. (*swing your elbows in time to the music*)

Mon-keys swing, mon-keys swing, Swing, swing, swing, swing, swing it, yeah!

2. (*swing your elbows in time to the music*)

Swing, swing, swing, swing, swing, those mon-keys can swing! Yeah!

1.

2.

These are first- and second-time bars.

Rhythm zone 2: slow-walk

Say and clap the rhythm below while a friend or teacher taps the beat, and then swap over. Remember to count and feel two beats for each 𝅗𝅥

'slow - walk'
minim (or half-note)

24 Classical sounds

Verse 1

Gracefully

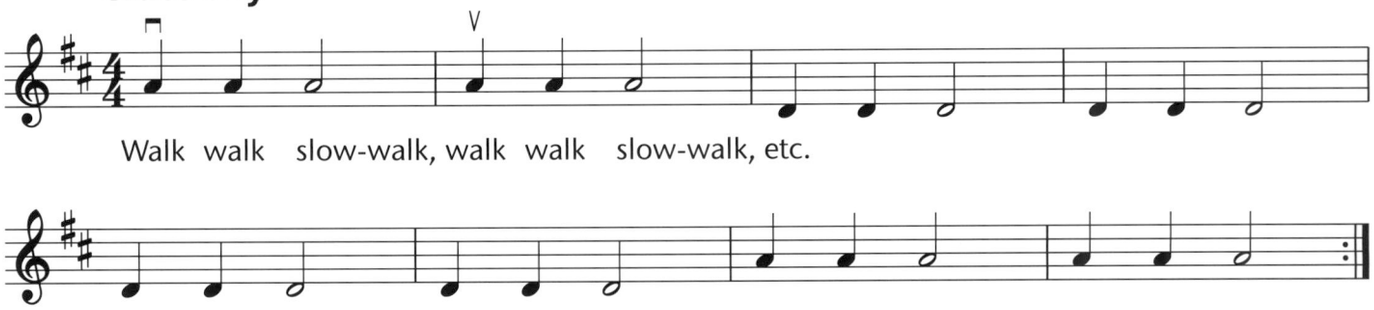

Verse 2

Verse 3

25 Super listener

Listen to track 25 and play 'Classical sounds' using your E and A strings. The first note will be open E.

Slow-walk tunes

26 Raindrops

Gently

Rain-drops fall from the sky, ground is wet, so am I.

On my head, on my knees, wish I had my wel - lies!

27 Swing band

Lively, swing

Swing your el - bow as you cross the string,

Swing your el - bow as you cross the string,

1. *Chant*

See - saw bow-ing, that's the thing! One more time now!

2. **Slower** trem.

thing! Swing it, yeah!

Remember Mr Tremolo!

Left-hand pizzicato

In these tunes you'll need to use left-hand pizzicato. When you see the + sign, pluck the string with your left-hand 4th finger.

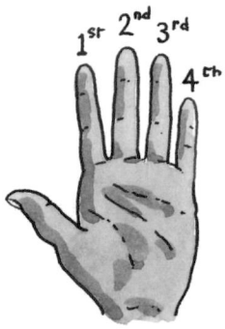

28 Chinese festival

Steadily

29 Popcorn

First sing the song and play left-hand pizzicato in the 'Pop! Bang!' bars. Then play with right-hand pizzicato or arco for the rest of the tune, but keep using your left hand for 'Pop! Bang!'.

Happily

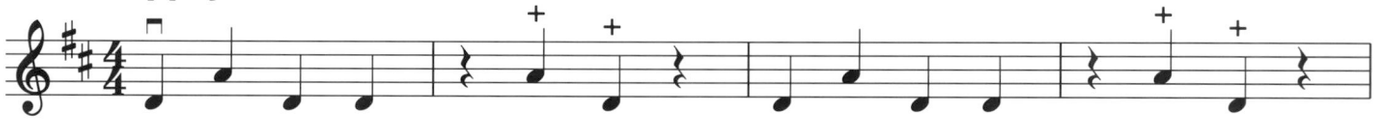

I like pop-corn, Pop! Bang! I like pop-corn, Pop! Bang!

I would like some, here's my mo - ney, salt or sweet, it's ve - ry yum - my.

I like pop-corn, Pop! Bang!

Finger jogging time

Four joggers

Say this rhyme and tap each fingertip in turn on your left-hand thumb.

4th finger:	Four	jog - gers	out	one	day,	one	fell	down	and	lost	his	way.
3rd finger:	Three	jog - gers	out	one	day,	one	fell	down	and	lost	his	way.
2nd finger:	Two	jog - gers	out	one	day,	one	fell	down	and	lost	his	way.
1st finger:	One	jog - ger	out	one	day,	he	fell	down	and	lost	his	way.
0 fingers:	No	jog - gers	out	to -	day!	(Stop!)						

30

Super listener

Listen to track 30 and play 'Four joggers' on your A string, starting with your 4th finger and lifting a finger off between each line.

Sporty rhythms

Shape up your left-hand fingers on the D string. Choose a sporty rhythm from below and play it on each fingered note and on the open D: 4–32–1–0. Make sure that your 2nd and 3rd fingers are close together.

Walk walk slow - walk,

Jog-ging walk jog-ging walk,

Rea - dy, stea - dy, go now,

Quick run - ner, fast sprint-er,

Also try playing up the notes from the open string: 0–1–23–4.

Finger jogging tunes

You can play these tunes on any string, but if you play with the CD, make sure you use the string shown.

31 Fingers and feet (D string)

4/4

22	22	33	33	22	22	11	11
From our	fingers	to our	feet, we	always	keep a	steady	beat, we
22	22	33	33	22	11	0	
keep it	going	in a	song if	notes are	short or	long_____.	

(Stamp feet eight times, then repeat.)

32 Roller coaster (D string)

4/4

3	3	22	22	11	11	0	0
Speed -	ing	roller	coaster,	spinning	me a -	round.	I'm
11	11	2	2	33	33	3	𝄽
feeling	very	diz -	zy	so far	from the	ground.	(rest)

(Make circles in the air with the bow, then repeat.)

33 String band (A string)

4/4

2	1	0	𝄽	2	1	0	𝄽
Big	cel -	los,	(rest)	big	cel -	los,	(rest)
00	00	11	11	2	1	0	𝄽 :‖
double	basses,	vio -	lins, and	big	cel -	los.	(rest)

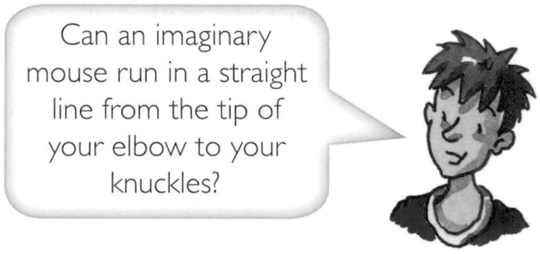

34 Rain, rain (A string)

35 Twinkle, twinkle, little star

This tune uses two different strings—a lower one and a higher one. CD track 35 is played on the D and A strings.

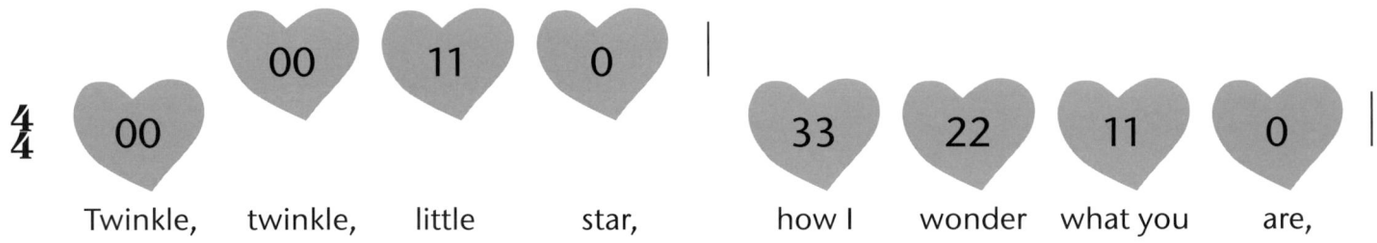

36 Super listener

Listen to track 36 and play 'Twinkle, twinkle, little star' starting on the A string.

Be a composer

Using the words below, make up your own tune using the left-hand fingers. Tap a steady beat and say the words through a few times before you start.

'Deep in the jungle, what do you see?
Alligators, alligators after me!'

D-string notes

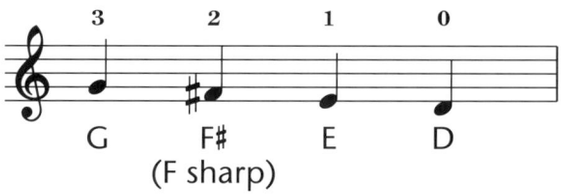

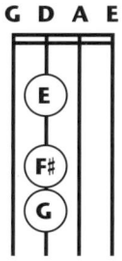

1st finger makes the note E

2nd finger makes the note F♯

3rd finger makes the note G

This is a sharp sign: ♯

37 This is G

38 Jogging in the city

Hold your 3rd finger down and be sure to leave an 'A-string tunnel'.

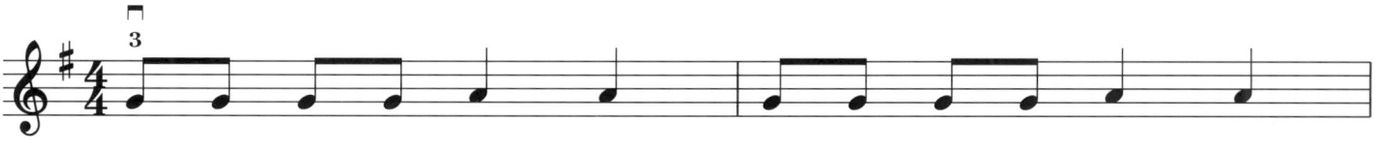

39 Perfect match

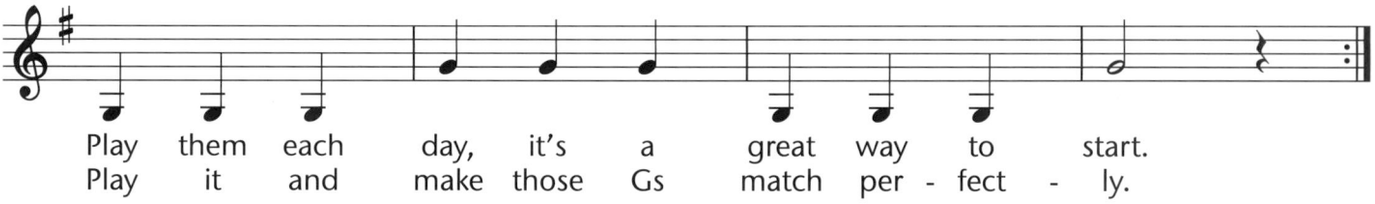

The sharps at the start of the music are called **key signatures**.

40 F sharp now

41 Venice and Vivaldi

Vivaldi, arr. KB/DB

42 Here comes E

43 Starlight

44 Super listener

Play 'Starlight' using the open A string and F♯ on the D string. Hold your 2nd finger down all the way through and let your open A string ring out clearly.

D-string activity page

Writing time

Draw these D-string notes on the stave below:

Bar 1: ♩ x 4 on open D

Bar 2: 𝅗𝅥 x 2 on E

Bar 3: ♩ 𝄽 ♩ 𝄽 on F♯

Bar 4: 𝅗𝅥 on G and a two-beat rest

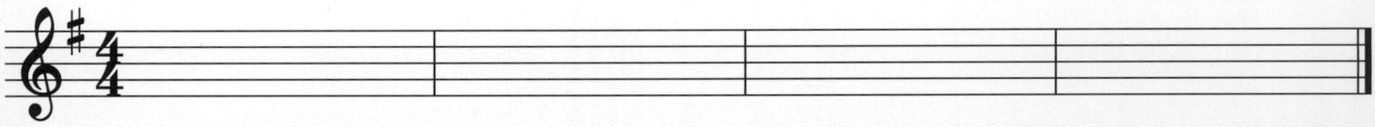

Now draw a down-bow sign above the first note and play the tune through.

Roller coaster quiz

Play 'Roller coaster' on page 24 and then do the quiz below.

- Some notes are missing in the tune. Fill them in where you see the * sign.
- Draw a circle around the time signature.
- Fill in the missing number: 4/4 means _____ ♩ beats in a bar.
- A ♩ rest is missing in bar 4. Draw it in correctly.
- Draw a circle around some ♫ Es.
- How many F♯s can you count in the first line? _____

45 Fit as a fiddle

Play the rhythm variations in verses 2 and 3 and end each verse with the chorus.

Verse 1

With energy

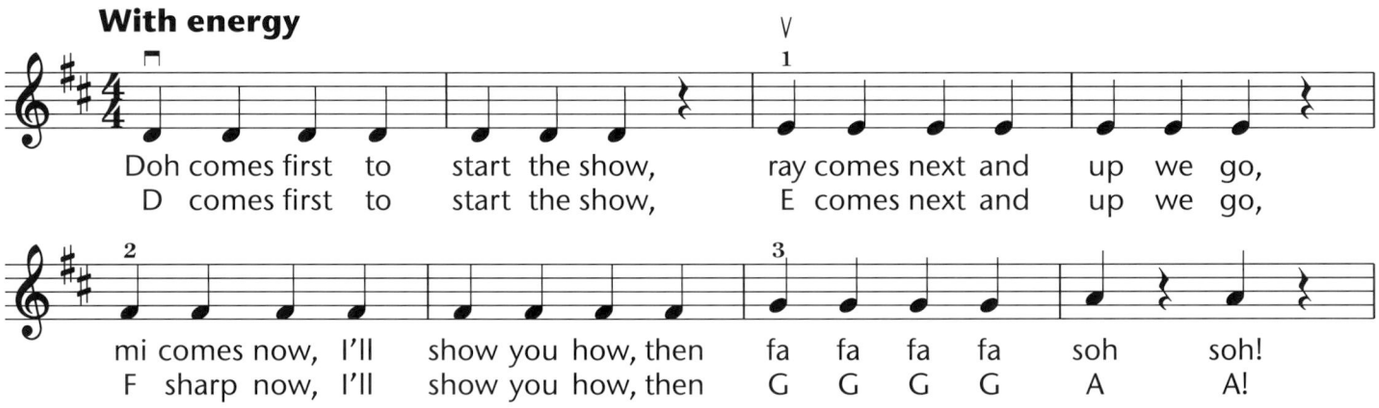

Chorus

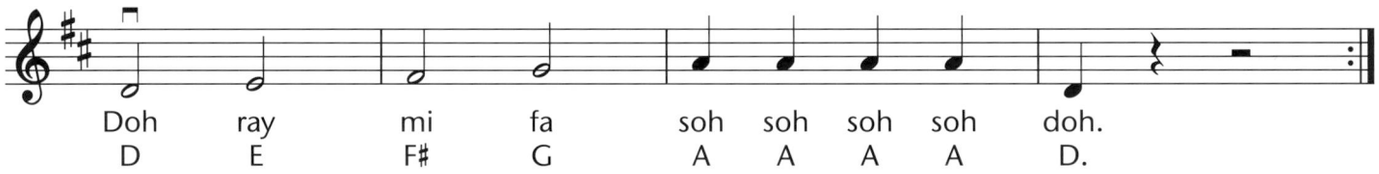

Verse 2

Verse 3

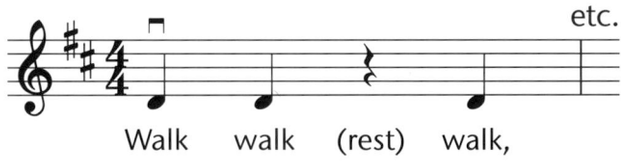

46 Finger-tapping cha-cha

Happily

Chant this as you tap your left-hand 3rd finger on the string:

Tap your finger, wiggle your thumb. Tap your finger, wiggle your thumb. Tap your finger, wiggle your thumb. Let's get ready, now here it comes. (*repeat the piece*)

47 Lost shoe blues

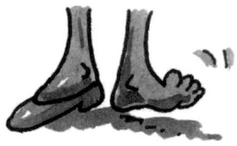

Play with a swing

G I'm blue, lost my shoe, don't know where I put it, got the

lost shoe blues. I'll miss the bus, what a fuss!

late for school and teach-er's mad, I feel so sad. I'll have to hop,

trem.

and not stop, don't know where I put it, got the lost shoe blues.

The next piece is in $\frac{2}{4}$.
What do you think that means?

48 Missed it!

On the move

Run-ning to the rail-way sta-tion, hope the train will be on time. I've

checked the time and des-tin-a-tion, it's on plat-form nine. Oh!

Train went past, it left with-out me, sped right down that rail-way line. I'm

stand-ing here at plat-form one, not plat-form num-ber nine!

At the end of the piece, slide your left hand up and down the fingerboard like a fast train.

A-string notes

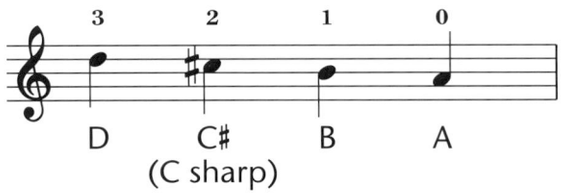

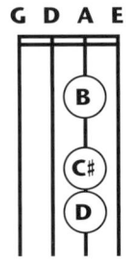

1st finger makes the note B

2nd finger makes the note C♯
3rd finger makes the note D

49 This is D

50 Super listener

Play 'Perfect match' on page 26 starting on your open D string.

51 C sharp now

52 Knock, knock!

Think of your favourite 'Knock, knock' jokes and play them using these notes.

53 Here comes B

54 Off to school

B can be written with the stem going up or down:

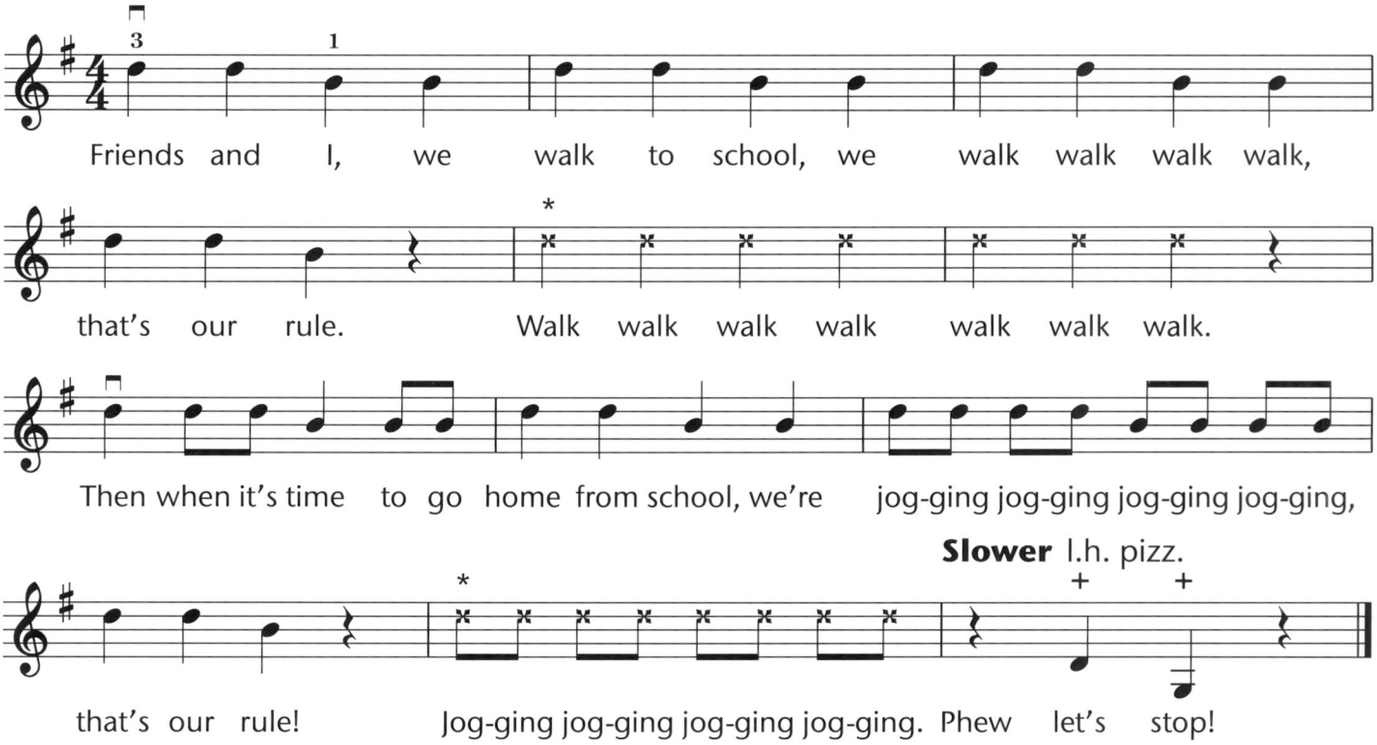

* Tap your 3rd finger on the A string.

55 Wake up!

A-string activity page

Writing time

Draw the A-string notes on the stave below. Each note will be a ♩

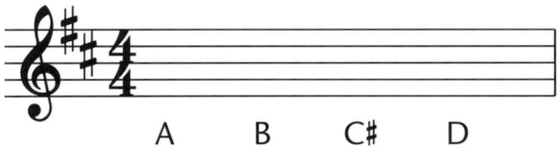

Be an A-string composer

Use the rhythm shown to write your own tune using the A-string notes. Choose one note per bar.

Now draw a down-bow sign above the first note and play your tune through.

56 Get aboard

Try some swinging rhythms in verses 2 and 3. Listen to track 56 to hear how it goes and get the swing of it!

Verse 1

Swinging along

Verse 2

Chickety-can, it goes speeding along, it goes
Chickety-can, it goes speeding along, it goes
Chickety-can, it goes speeding along, it goes
Chickety-can all day long!

Verse 3

Speeding here and speeding there, it
Speeds right down the railway track, it's
Speeding here and speeding there, don't
Know when we'll be back!

57 Clear blue sky

Gently

Harmonic-ky things

Octave harmonics: to find this special sound, touch the string very lightly about halfway along with your 4th finger. This is the harmonic sign: ○

58 Harmonic-ky thing

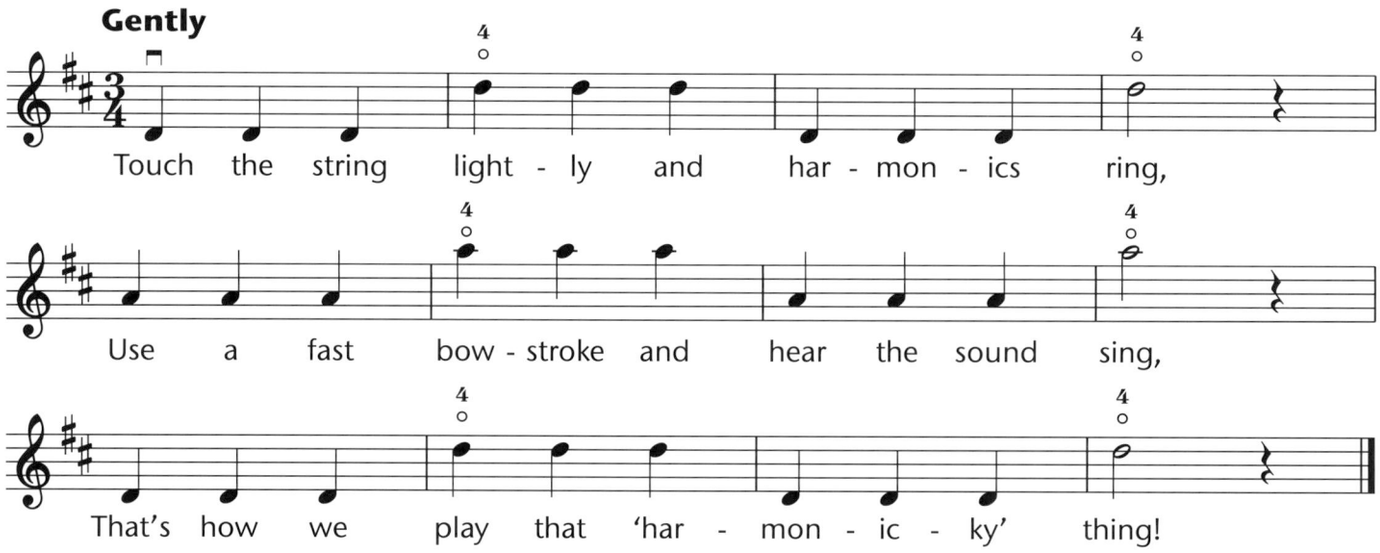

59 Emma's lullaby

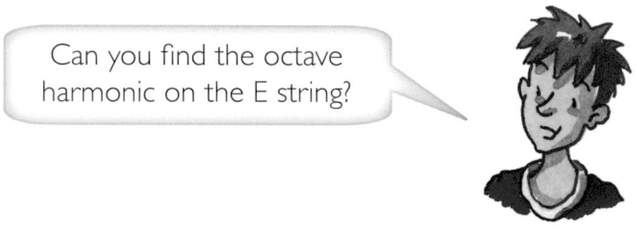

Clear blue sky

Play this harmonic part while your friend or teacher plays the tune on the opposite page, then swap over. Use track 57 on the CD.

Scale-y things

60 Scale builder

Listen — *Copy*

Can you play the D-string notes and co - py me? Doh ray mi fa. Doh ray mi fa.
D E F♯ G. D E F♯ G.

Listen — *Copy*

Now play the A string, but lis-ten first to me: Soh la ti doh. Soh la ti doh.
A B C♯ D. A B C♯ D.

Listen — *Play together*

Can you play the scale of D a - long with me? Doh ray mi fa soh la ti doh.
D E F♯ G A B C♯ D.

Listen — *Play together*

Let's play the whole scale to - ge-ther, you and me: Doh ray mi fa soh la ti doh.
D E F♯ G A B C♯ D.

Listen — *Play together*

We have played a scale to - ge-ther now. That's it!

Scale-y dragon

Choose an idea from the scale-y dragon and play a scale of D major in that way. Make up some more ideas of your own.

Scale of D major

Play a different rhythm for each note of the scale.

Play $\frac{4}{4}$ rhythms with track 61. Play $\frac{3}{4}$ rhythms with track 62.

63 Aiming high

Confidently

Play 'Aiming high' as a round. The second part enters at *.

Super listener

Play a scale starting on your G or A string.

64 G major $\frac{3}{4}$ 65 A major $\frac{4}{4}$

66 Souallé

Like a lullaby

Lul - la - by, sweet dreams to-night, etc.

Slower (2nd time only)

(**1** 2 3, **1** 2 3, **1** 2 3)

67 Snap!

Creepy

arco

Sca - ly skin, ra - zor teeth, prowl - ing for his lunch,

Look - ing for some-thing sweet, some-thing he can crunch.

If he comes creep - ing near, don't be too po - lite,

Fine

Cro - co - diles al - ways smile, but they like to bite.

pizz.

D.C. al Fine

Snap, snap, snap! Snap, snap, snap! Snap, snap, snap! Snap, snap, snap!

D.C. al Fine means repeat from the start and stop at the word **Fine**.

68 More Mini Mozart

Gracefully

Try these rhythm variations:

69 Hide and seek

On the move

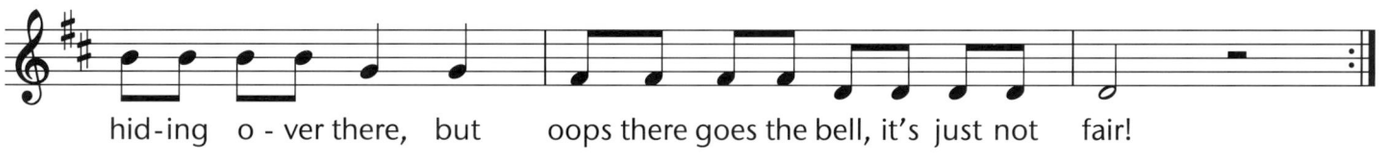

70 Beach holiday